Walking in your Truth

A PERSONAL JOURNAL
TO REFLECT ON YOUR LIFE'S PURPOSE

ALICIA ADAMSON

Walk in your truth!

Walking In Your Truth Journal
ISBN-13:978-0692799222
ISBN-10:0692799222

Book Design: sharonbrewsterdesign.com
Alicia Adamson's Photo: danitajo.com

THIS JOURNAL IS DEDICATED TO
*my Mother Pam, my late Grandmother Geneva,
my husband Kasim and our sons, Kasim, Jr. and Jordan,
for empowering me to live my truth and loving me
unconditionally flaws and all!*

Walking in your Truth

A PERSONAL JOURNAL
TO REFLECT ON YOUR LIFE'S PURPOSE

ALICIA ADAMSON

Edited by: Kimberly Y. Jones

I PROMISE

to discover, accept and tell the truth, the whole truth,
and nothing but the truth so that I can walk boldly in my truth.

_____

Signature

Dear Truth Seeker,

Journaling is a powerful tool to self-discovery, healing and empowerment. I have used journaling since I was a child to record and attempt to process my feelings in a safe place to a safe person, ME! Life expects us to always have it together, to be and appear strong, to wear "the mask" 24/7 and never complain about it. Truth be told, most of us are living someone else's life, someone else's truth. Not because we dislike our own lives, somehow we have believed that we are not worthy of truth but of lies. We don't even know what the truth looks like because it has all been laid out for us in some form or fashion. Who we should be, who we should date, how we should react, how we should talk, look and navigate this thing called life. Our lives are set up to pacify each other, but most people won't call us out because they are too busy trying to survive the lies.

When was the last time someone told you the real truth about you? I'll wait...

How did it land, did it hurt? Did it make you upset? Did you even listen? We aren't socialized to hear truth, only accept lies. Lies make us feel comfortable, they paint a picture that is safe, a picture that is controllable. If we can control the outcome, then we are living our best lives huh? Sounds familiar?

I learned the hard way that to leave my life's truth up to the standards and perspectives of others would lead me to a meaningless life. Until I learned *Whose* I was, I didn't know Who I was. When I look back, I spent so many years searching...in silence. My life appeared fun, fulfilled, successful but it wasn't until I had a moment of truth with myself and God that I realized my life was not in my hands! I spent my entire teenage and early twenties chronicling my life, not because I was this amazing aspiring writer with plans to live in a remote location and write forever — it was my therapy. Not so much Dear Diary, more like Dear God. I had so much to say, so many feelings to release. I didn't trust anyone with my inner most feelings — such as self-doubt, failure, fear, pain, unrequited love and unworthiness. You know, the deep stuff.

Journaling saved me from self-destruction. My healing did not come from the counsel of my close girlfriends, my mother or any love interest. Journaling was a creative platform to my healing. I had to lay aside any and all shame in order to start this process. I had to stand toe to toe with fear and wrestle for my life — my true life.

I can go on and on about my life, but this is not about me! I'm a firm believer that everything that has happened to me for a reason and it has all worked in my favor! This has been a two-year project, a process in itself!

This journal is structured in three parts — Part One, I will introduce you to self-reflection and facilitate the process of growth for you to begin your walk. Take your time and work at a pace that feels most comfortable. Part Two, will guide you through a seven day consecutive journal process to increase your level of introspection. Part Three, the final phase, is designed for you to take what you've learned and it apply it to your personal journaling. Be free, be vulnerable, be you!

You chose this book because you are at a crossroads in your life where you are ready to tell your truth. My hope is that you use this journal to initiate an intimate conversation between your mind, heart and your soul so that you can move forward in truth in all areas of your life. We are all searching for our divine purpose, but in order to find it, you have to walk in your truth!

PART I
SEVEN LESSONS IN TRUTH

No more lies

Think about your story — the narrative that plays like a movie reel in your mind over and over. It's the story you tell your friends about why you are the way you are, or the story you tell the love of your life about why you love so hard. Perhaps it's the way you portray your life right now — social media is filled with picture perfect poses, you dress in tailored clothes, possess multiple degrees, power couple, luxury car… You have the imagery. Are you happy? Is your life fulfilled?

Now let's tell the real truth. Identify at least three lies in your story. Why do you lie about these things? Is the truth more painful than the lie? If so, why? What shame do you carry with these lies and what scares you about your truth? Who benefits from your lies? Who suffers for your truths? Now identify at least three truths to counter the lies you previously told.

THE LIES

1. _____
2. _____
3. _____

THE TRUTHS

1. _____
2. _____
3. _____

Coach Note: Spend as much time as you want, or need, on this truth. It may take you some time to think through this entry. You may stop and come back to it, you may cry and get frustrated, you may easily complete this in one sitting. Stretch yourself, get comfortable being uncomfortable.

_____

_____

_____

_____

_____

_____

_____

_____

_____

_____

_____

_____

_____

_____

_____

_____

_____

_____

_____

_____

_____

_____

_____

_____

_____

_____

LESSON TWO
Self-Check

Take this time to free write answers to the questions below:

How are you feeling today? What is going well in your life?
What/Who brings you joy?

What are you most of proud of?

Let's go deeper... What are you most ashamed of? What don't you want people to know about you?

What is your greatest fear? What have you been hurt/angry about all these years that you just can't let go?

_____

_____

_____

_____

_____

_____

_____

_____

_____

_____

_____

Coach Note: It is so important to stop and think about how you are doing! Checking in with you is essential to your personal growth and ensuring that you always know what's going on with you before anyone else has to tell you! Schedule a self-check at least every 3 to 4 months. Write a journal entry on where you are with you at the present time. You will be surprised at how much you've been holding in.

_____

_____

_____

_____

_____

_____

_____

_____

_____

_____

_____

_____

_____

_____

_____

_____

_____

_____

_____

LESSON THREE
Family Un-Ties

Family can be complicated. We all come from different family structures equipped with their own lies, secrets, chaos and dysfunctions! But how do these ugly truths affect you and how you view yourself? How do unhealthy family relationships get in the way of your personal and professional growth? Take the time to painfully examine those who are often times closest and dearest to you. Is it time to self-preserve and un-tie from family members who are barriers to your truth?

_____

_____

_____

_____

_____

_____

_____

_____

_____

_____

_____

_____

_____

Coach Note: Blood is not always thicker than water. In fact, blood can sometimes suffocate your growth. For those of you who are blessed with perfect families, shout-out to you! But those of us who know our families are in need of some makeovers, then you need to understand this fundamental truth about family — sometimes you have to love from afar. Never let anyone or anything hinder you from being who you are supposed to be.

_____

_____

_____

_____

_____

_____

_____

_____

_____

_____

_____

_____

_____

_____

_____

_____

_____

_____

_____

_____

_____

_____

_____

_____

LESSON FOUR

Sometimes you just have to Cry.
And Cry…. And Cry until something happens.

Give yourself space and time to cry. Crying is often viewed as a weakness, but God gave us tears for a reason, crying is a stress reliever. The act calms the body and sends your lungs into a breathing pattern that is calming. So treat your body well and cry! You must go there now — those sad things, those hurtful things, those experiences that cut so deep you choose to push them down. It's time to cry about them so that you can heal. Take all the time you need…

Now write about that experience, how did you feel? Did it feel natural, weird, good, bad, etc.?

_____

_____

_____

_____

_____

_____

_____

_____

_____

_____

Coach Note: Healing from the inside out starts with a bold cry. Stop holding in the very emotion that is pushing to get out. Crying is not for the weak, but for the strong and the wise. It's exhilarating and helps you release what you want to remain repressed. So here's what we are going to do together. Let's do the ugly cry. I want you to feel empowered and strong because you have embraced crying on your journey of truth!

_____

_____

_____

_____

_____

_____

_____

_____

_____

_____

_____

_____

_____

_____

_____

_____

_____

_____

Forgive Seventy Times Seventy

Forgiving others can be very hard and if we are being truthful, it's not something that we willingly seek to do. How do you forgive someone who has hurt you deeply? Forgiveness begins with activating love. Real love is unconditional. We are not capable of love if we cannot practice forgiveness as a lifestyle. It's time for you to forgive a few people. Take the next hour to journal about at least four people you need to forgive and why. Try to reflect on the process of making this list of people, the thought of forgiving them and how you see yourself feeling after you decide to forgive. Take as much time as you need with this journal entry, don't rush it.

_____

_____

_____

_____

_____

_____

_____

_____

_____

_____

_____

_____

_____

_____

Coach Note: Whether it's your mother, father, siblings, a best friend or former lover, find a way to Forgive! This process is not about the offender but about you, we all deserve to give and receive forgiveness. When we hold on to all the wrongs people have done to us, we block out all the blessings that are waiting. It's not easy so I plead with you stretch yourself to forgive the unforgivable and watch how your life changes.

LESSON SIX
Love does not hurt

If someone loves you, it should never hurt. They will not hurt you emotionally, verbally or physically. That is not to say people are perfect, there is a difference between deliberate infliction of pain and making mistakes that unintentionally hurt. Love inspires, ignites, heals, covers, celebrates, and is unselfish. No one who says they love you in your life has permission to treat you less than what you deserve, but unfortunately we allow people into our lives who don't deserve to be there. Think and then write about some people in your life whose love does not reflect what love should be. Journal about why you allow them to lease negative space in your life? Do you know what kind of love you are worthy of and deserve or are you still searching? Be honest with what's hindering you from receiving real love.

_____

_____

_____

_____

_____

_____

_____

_____

_____

_____

_____

_____

Coach Note: So many people stay on the lie journey because they are surrounded by hateful people who claim to love them. We often don't know enough about what we deserve and because of that, we don't hold others accountable. To love and receive love is an honor. Not everyone is equipped to participate in this action. Don't expect people who don't love themselves to love you. Watch what they do, hear not what they say. Demand that friends, family and romantic partners give you the love you deserve. Why? Because you deserve it.

Lesson Seven
What do you believe in?

In a world that is filled with so many conflicting values, beliefs and stances, I ask you to ask yourself what you believe in and why. What we believe influences our everyday life whether know it or not! Take some time to reflect and journal about the following questions: What do you stand for in this life? Do you believe you were created for a divine purpose? Do you believe that you are right where you are supposed to be and that everything that you have been through and are going through will manifest into something greater?

_____

_____

_____

_____

_____

_____

_____

_____

_____

Coach Note: I believe in God, I have hope humanity will overcome hate and I have faith that all things work for my good! My life has joy because my foundation is rooted in my faith. Life can be hard, confusing, chaotic, heartbreaking, lonely and downright unfair. In my late teens, I was called back to my faith because I was searching to fill the hole that we all have with the wrong things. There is a saying — "when you know whose you are, you know who you are"— I found me through God. We were all created for a divine purpose, this thing called life is full of opportunities for your purpose to be fulfilled, you've just got to tap in to the source of it all. Challenge your mind to think with your heart and your soul, you cannot intellectualize belief, it's something you feel.

_____

_____

_____

_____

_____

_____

_____

_____

_____

_____

_____

_____

_____

_____

_____

_____

_____

_____

_____

_____

_____

_____

_____

Part II
Seven Days of Truth

For the next seven days, we will commit and dedicate time to journal.
We won't stay stuck in what's happening to us, but instead focus on
what's happening for us and how we can learn more about who we are.
Refrain from social media, socializing and overall distractions.
Give yourself an emotional and spiritual vacation to just focus on you.

DAY ONE:
Truth Day

Knowing the truth about you will help you envision yourself with clarity and understanding. Most times we are stuck between who we were and who we are that we cannot see who we were created to be and how important it is to reach our full potential. You were created for greatness! Take the time to reflect and write a narrative about your truth journey. Self-discovery. The good , bad and ugly.

WHO YOU WERE

_____

_____

WHO YOU ARE

_____

_____

WHO YOU WERE CREATED TO BE

_____

_____

Coach Note: I believe in God, I have hope humanity will overcome hate and I have faith that all things work for my good! My life has joy because my foundation is rooted in my faith. Life can be hard, confusing, chaotic, heartbreaking, lonely and downright unfair. In my late teens, I was called back to my faith because I was searching to fill the hole that we all have with the wrong things. There is a saying — "when you know whose you are, you know who you are"— I found me through God. We were all created for a divine purpose, this thing called life is full of opportunities for your purpose to be fulfilled, you've just got to tap in to the source of it all. Challenge your mind to think with your heart and your soul, you cannot intellectualize belief, it's something you feel.

WALKING IN YOUR TRUTH

_____

_____

_____

_____

_____

_____

_____

_____

_____

_____

_____

_____

_____

_____

_____

_____

_____

_____

_____

_____

_____

_____

_____

DAY TWO:
Dear Me

This is going to be a tough day, not because you can't overcome this exercise but because you may become frustrated with how to begin, but it's OK, DON'T PANIC, it's all part of the process. Think back to when you were 17 years old, the crossroad between being a teenager and becoming a young adult. Were there experiences that happened to you that require closure? Now is the time to heal. Write a letter to your 17-year old self. Tell your truths — everything that your younger self should know and offer forgiveness and empathy when necessary.

DEAR ME,

_____

_____

_____

_____

_____

_____

_____

_____

_____

_____

_____

_____

Coach Note: Give yourself a moment to pat yourself on the back for getting through this letter. Not so bad huh! Did you feel free and a sense of relief after? Sometimes we need to go back and heal our younger self because at times they still exist within our adult lives. Recognizing this connection helps us to grow and stand confidently in our truth. This exercise is powerful because you realize that you are a survivor! Everything worked for your good!

_____

_____

_____

_____

_____

_____

_____

_____

_____

_____

_____

_____

_____

_____

_____

_____

_____

_____

_____

_____

_____

_____

_____

DAY THREE:
Moving Forward

Yesterday's entry should make today's much easier! Hopefully you cried, laughed and hopefully forgave yourself for being imperfect! The truth of the matter is we will often forgive others before we decide to forgive ourselves. During one of my speaking engagements, I asked the audience do they understand this concept of forgiving oneself — and the reply was no. Because society does not teach us to do this, we are told to forgive others but not ourselves. It's a skill that we don't have however, an essential tool that we all need. I learned at an early age that Love and Forgiveness are two of the most powerful expressions of humanity, yet the hardest to do. It requires vulnerability, accessibility and accountability. Give yourself the gift of forgiveness. This exercise is dedicated to teaching you how and what to forgive yourself for.

FINISH THIS FORGIVENESS STATEMENT:
I FORGIVE ME FOR...

_____

_____

_____

_____

_____

I will no longer hold myself hostage to my past and my inability to let go and honor myself with forgiveness. I know these things are still hurting me and the longer I allow them to hurt me, the longer I will stay in this place of being stuck in my own mess. When I learn to forgive me, I'm giving myself permission to make mistakes, to not always make the right choices and to not always be as wise as I'd like to think I am. Forgiving myself gives me the opportunity to empower myself, trust myself more, and trust those around me. I forgive me forever and ever.

Coach Note: Self forgiveness is more powerful than you think. Never forgive anyone before you forgive yourself. Extend grace and mercy to yourself first. After you forgive you, then you can forgive others. Don't discount this simple, yet difficult task in your daily life.

_____

_____

_____

_____

_____

_____

_____

_____

_____

_____

_____

_____

_____

_____

_____

_____

_____

_____

_____

_____

_____

_____

DAY FOUR:
Imagine Me

"Write the vision and make it plain on tablets that he may run who reads it"
— *Habakkuk 2:2*

Creating your vision on paper will hold your dreams accountable to becoming reality. It's like building a house without a blueprint — there will be a lack of synergy! Take this time to think about how your spiritual, professional and personal life will collide with destiny and steer your life the right way. Use words and pictures that represent you. Take the time to be creative and dream.

INSTRUCTIONS:
Create a visual representation of where you see your life in the next 1-3 years, after you create this board, write a journal entry about your process and how you plan to stay accountable to it. *What you will need: Favorite Magazines, scissors, glue, tape, markers and poster board (whatever size works for your vision).*

_____

_____

_____

_____

_____

_____

_____

_____

_____

Coach Note: My vision board hasn't changed since I made it five years ago. It hangs at my desk at work where I can stare at it every day. It's a holistic picture of who I am spiritually, emotionally and professionally. The things I value most are reflected on the vision board and it reminds me to keep dreaming. Dare to boldly share your truth visually and watch how your life begins to take shape!

_____

_____

_____

_____

_____

_____

_____

_____

_____

_____

_____

_____

_____

_____

_____

_____

_____

_____

DAY FIVE:
The Gift Box

We were all given unique gifts and talents according to our purpose. However, we don't all use our gifts, in fact, we hold back our gifts out of fear of rejection, jealously, judgment and feeling "too" special. Walking boldly in your truth starts with recognizing and activating your gifts to the highest level and not being ashamed of how talented you are! This next exercise will be fun! It will require some thinking as it relates to the gifts that are known to you, perhaps you may decide to consult people who know you really well and ask them what they think you're really good at doing. It's OK to take a poll of others because sometimes we don't see ourselves the way others do, especially the way God sees us.

Coach Note: Create a platform for your gifts or else they will stay boxed up inside forever! Be proud of your super powers. Your gifts are not about you; someone is waiting to receive your gifts to help their life. If you find that you are in an atmosphere that does not receive your gifts, then it's time to move on from that place.

INSTRUCTIONS:

Inside the box below write down the gifts and the talents you have and on the outside list the gifts that you share with others, whether it is through your job, your church, your family, etc. Reflect on how you feel when you are exercising your gifts, do you feel whole? Proud? On mission/purpose? For those of you who have hidden your gifts, ask yourself why? What fears do you have?

DAY SIX:
Shout-outs to ME!

Give yourself a pat on the back, high five, an extra cherry on top and more for all of the great steps forward you have accomplished! You don't need to wait for other people to celebrate and give you validation for what you bring to the table. Do it yourself and own your shout-outs because nobody knows you like you!

_____

_____

_____

_____

_____

_____

_____

_____

_____

_____

_____

_____

_____

_____

_____

_____

Coach Note: This society tells us that we are narcissists or conceited if we talk highly of ourselves too much. There is a healthy balance and an art to this. This problem is we've gone so far to the left that many of us feel bad about giving ourselves accolades. There is nothing wrong with you telling yourself, "Job well done!" Studies show that people who participate in daily affirmations are authentically confident and tend to lead a joyful life.

MAKE A LIST:

List at least 10 shout-outs that you should be excited about and then write
a journal entry about this process of giving yourself praise and how you plan
to stay accountable to being the first to give you shout-outs!

1. *Girl you are* _____

2. *You were so fierce during* _____

3. *You really look* _____

4. *Good job on* _____

5. *You are amazing at* _____

6. *When I walk in the room* _____

7. *I'm so blessed because* _____

8. *I'm extremely good at* _____

9. *It comes natural to me to* _____

10. *People usually lean on me for* _____

_____

_____

_____

_____

_____

_____

_____

_____

DAY SEVEN:
Personal Reflection

Seven lessons of truth and a seven-day crash course in journaling about you.
What have you learned about yourself during this process and how has this process
made you feel. Did you get to some truths about you, if so what were? If you did not
reach any truths, reflect on why? What exercises made you the most comfortable
and which ones did not? What exercise(s) helped you achieve the most growth?
As we close out this seven-day truth journey the most important exercise is this one.
Take this time to be vulnerable and connect all the dots that you started plotting
throughout this book.

_____

_____

_____

_____

_____

_____

_____

_____

_____

_____

_____

_____

*Coach Note: Introspection is a gift! Many of us want to speed ahead to the product but don't
want to go through the process. Schedule time with yourself to always to check in with you.
Journaling provides you the space to slow down and reflect on your progress. Take the time
to pat yourself on the back for the wins and focus on how you can learn from the losses.
This is not a one and done! This is an ongoing commitment to personal development
and a belief that walking through life in your own truth is the only way you want to live!*

_____

_____

_____

_____

_____

_____

_____

_____

_____

_____

_____

_____

_____

_____

_____

_____

_____

_____

_____

_____

_____

_____

_____

_____

Part III
Your Truth

The final section of this journal is blank intentionally!
You've done great work thus far and now it's time to apply what you
learned through your truth journey. Use this space to write your thoughts,
Illustrate your feelings and chronicle your growth from day to day.
Extra exercises on the following page are there to help you started.

Additional Journal Exercises

SPIRITUAL WELLNESS

Write a prayer, petition about what you are grateful for, what you hope for yourself and for others.

ACCOUNTABILITY

How are you holding the people close to you accountable? What are your deal breakers? Everyone should have some. As my mother used to say, "If you don't stand for something, you will fall for everything." What issues are you standing your ground on or what issues should you be standing your ground on?

DO SOMETHING COMPLETELY OUT OF THE BOX, OR OUTSIDE YOUR COMFORT ZONE THAT MAKES YOU VULNERABLE

Take yourself out on a date, go to a movie alone, take a safe weekend trip to another city or state you have always wanted to visit, bungee jump, or whatever you have been delaying doing for yourself, even if you must do it by yourself. What's that thing you have always wanted to do? Take advantage of the opportunity to do it and journal your experience the entire time.

PRESS THE YES BUTTON

If you did not have to ask for permission to be who you were created to be, what would you be doing?

GIVE YOURSELF AWAY

Do something for someone else, volunteer at a local nonprofit, a food bank, day shelter or teen center. How grateful are you for your own life? What can you do to give back to others so that your life is not always centered around you? Giving back is essential to one's growth because it takes the focus off our nature to be selfish and demands us to lead with our hearts.

ALICIA ADAMSON

_____
_____
_____
_____
_____
_____
_____
_____
_____
_____
_____
_____
_____
_____
_____
_____
_____
_____

"Sometimes you got to let the tears fall. They fall because you are grateful for the grace and mercy in your life. They fall to remind of you of just how far you have journeyed. They remind you that everything is going to be OK and that you are more than a conqueror, you are a survivor!"

ALICIA ADAMSON

_____

_____

_____

_____

_____

_____

_____

_____

_____

_____

_____

_____

_____

_____

_____

_____

_____

_____

_____

_____

_____

_____

_____

Forgiveness = Freedom

ALICIA ADAMSON

_____
_____
_____
_____
_____
_____
_____
_____
_____
_____
_____
_____
_____
_____
_____
_____
_____
_____
_____
_____

"The Truth Journey is lonely, you are unpacking along the way,
shedding off people and experiences that are not allowed on your destiny trip!
Stop trying to drag them along. This is your unique journey alone."

ALICIA ADAMSON

_____

_____

_____

_____

_____

_____

_____

_____

_____

_____

_____

_____

_____

_____

_____

_____

_____

_____

_____

_____

*"Love starts with me. I have to teach people how to love me
and hold them accountable because I'm worth it."*

ALICIA ADAMSON

_____

_____

_____

_____

_____

_____

_____

_____

_____

_____

_____

_____

_____

_____

_____

_____

_____

_____

_____

_____

_____

_____

*"Love starts with me. I have to teach people how to love me
and hold them accountable because I'm worth it."*

ALICIA ADAMSON

"Stop lying about how you're really living — truth be told you are suffering in silence, dying inside, not wanting to reveal how you really feel about your life at this moment. You have permission to tell your truth and not look back again."

ALICIA ADAMSON

_"Fear is a real imaginary friend. It tries to convince you how real it is
and will try to cling to every new experience you want to do. I've learned to say,
"OK Fear, if you won't leave on your own, I'll just drag you along with me because
you're not going to stop me from going where I need to go.'"_

ALICIA ADAMSON

_____

_____

_____

_____

_____

_____

_____

_____

_____

_____

_____

_____

_____

_____

_____

_____

_____

_____

_____

_____

_____

_____

"Truth: You are equipped with everything you will ever need to face the successes and challenges in your life. If you just walk in who you are, you will win!"

_____

_____

_____

_____

_____

_____

_____

_____

_____

_____

_____

_____

_____

_____

_____

_____

_____

_____

_____

_____

_____

_____

_____

"Sometimes we have to love family members from afar.
If anyone interrupts our peace, they cannot stay."

ALICIA ADAMSON

_____
_____
_____
_____
_____
_____
_____
_____
_____
_____
_____
_____
_____
_____
_____
_____
_____
_____
_____
_____
_____
_____
_____
_____

"Every wound that has been healed, every tear that has been dried,
every need that has been met is all due to my personal relationship with God.
He has favored me and allowed me to have an abundant life.
My joy is because of Him only."

_____
_____
_____
_____
_____
_____
_____
_____
_____
_____
_____
_____
_____
_____
_____
_____
_____
_____
_____
_____
_____
_____

WALKING IN YOUR TRUTH

"Life is intertwined, you cannot succeed in your professional life,
if you personally life is not solid and vice versa. I believe true authenticity comes
when there is a perfect intersection between your personal, spiritual and professional life.
That's the True you."

WALKING IN YOUR TRUTH

"Truth is we all tell lies about who we are because we have been told we are not good enough just the way we are. This world has no authority over you or your destiny. You are free to authentically and unapologetically walk in your truth."

ALICIA ADAMSON

_____

_____

_____

_____

_____

_____

_____

_____

_____

_____

_____

_____

_____

_____

_____

_____

_____

_____

_____

_____

_____

"Sometimes you got to let the tears fall. They fall because you are grateful for the grace and mercy in your life. They fall to remind of you of just how far you have journeyed. They remind you that everything is going to be OK and that you are more than a conqueror, you are a survivor!"

ALICIA ADAMSON

_____

_____

_____

_____

_____

_____

_____

_____

_____

_____

_____

_____

_____

_____

_____

_____

_____

_____

Forgiveness = Freedom

ALICIA ADAMSON

_____

_____

_____

_____

_____

_____

_____

_____

_____

_____

_____

_____

_____

_____

_____

_____

_____

_____

_____

_____

_____

"The Truth Journey is lonely, you are unpacking along the way,
shedding off people and experiences that are not allowed on your destiny trip!
Stop trying to drag them along. This is your unique journey alone."

ALICIA ADAMSON

WALKING IN YOUR TRUTH

---

*"Love starts with me. I have to teach people how to love me
and hold them accountable because I'm worth it."*

WALKING IN YOUR TRUTH

_____

_____

_____

_____

_____

_____

_____

_____

_____

_____

_____

_____

_____

_____

_____

_____

_____

_____

_____

_____

_____

_____

*"Love starts with me. I have to teach people how to love me
and hold them accountable because I'm worth it."*

ALICIA ADAMSON

_____

_____

_____

_____

_____

_____

_____

_____

_____

_____

_____

_____

_____

_____

_____

_____

_____

_____

_____

_____

_____

_____

_____

_____

_____

"Stop lying about how you're really living — truth be told you are suffering in silence,
dying inside, not wanting to reveal how you really feel about your life at this moment.
You have permission to tell your truth and not look back again."

ALICIA ADAMSON

_____

_____

_____

_____

_____

_____

_____

_____

_____

_____

_____

_____

_____

_____

_____

_____

_____

_____

_____

_____

_____

_____

_____

*"Fear is a real imaginary friend. It tries to convince you how real it is
and will try to cling to every new experience you want to do. I've learned to say,
"OK Fear, if you won't leave on your own, I'll just drag you along with me because
you're not going to stop me from going where I need to go.'"*

ALICIA ADAMSON

_____

_____

_____

_____

_____

_____

_____

_____

_____

_____

_____

_____

_____

_____

_____

_____

_____

_____

_____

_____

_____

_____

_____

"Truth: You are equipped with everything you will ever need to face the successes and challenges in your life. If you just walk in who you are, you will win!"

ALICIA ADAMSON

_____

_____

_____

_____

_____

_____

_____

_____

_____

_____

_____

_____

_____

_____

_____

_____

_____

_____

_____

_____

_____

_____

"Sometimes we have to love family members from afar.
If anyone interrupts our peace, they cannot stay."

ALICIA ADAMSON

_____

_____

_____

_____

_____

_____

_____

_____

_____

_____

_____

_____

_____

_____

_____

_____

_____

_____

_____

_____

"Every wound that has been healed, every tear that has been dried,
every need that has been met is all due to my personal relationship with God.
He has favored me and allowed me to have an abundant life.
My joy is because of Him only."

_____

_____

_____

_____

_____

_____

_____

_____

_____

_____

_____

_____

_____

_____

_____

_____

_____

_____

_____

_____

"Life is intertwined, you cannot succeed in your professional life,
if you personally life is not solid and vice versa. I believe true authenticity comes
when there is a perfect intersection between your personal, spiritual and professional life.
That's the True you."

ALICIA ADAMSON

_____

_____

_____

_____

_____

_____

_____

_____

_____

_____

_____

_____

_____

_____

_____

_____

_____

_____

_____

_____

_____

_____

*"Truth is we all tell lies about who we are because we have been told we are
not good enough just the way we are. This world has no authority over you or your destiny.
You are free to authentically and unapologetically walk in your truth."*

ALICIA ADAMSON

_"Sometimes you got to let the tears fall. They fall because you are grateful for
the grace and mercy in your life. They fall to remind of you of just how far you have journeyed.
They remind you that everything is going to be OK and that you are
more than a conqueror, you are a survivor!"_

ALICIA ADAMSON

Forgiveness = Freedom

ALICIA ADAMSON

_____

_____

_____

_____

_____

_____

_____

_____

_____

_____

_____

_____

_____

_____

_____

_____

_____

_____

_____

_____

_____

_____

_____

_____

_____

*"The Truth Journey is lonely, you are unpacking along the way,
shedding off people and experiences that are not allowed on your destiny trip!
Stop trying to drag them along. This is your unique journey alone."*

ALICIA ADAMSON

_____

_____

_____

_____

_____

_____

_____

_____

_____

_____

_____

_____

_____

_____

_____

_____

_____

_____

_____

_____

_____

_____

_____

_____

"Love starts with me. I have to teach people how to love me
and hold them accountable because I'm worth it."

_____

_____

_____

_____

_____

_____

_____

_____

_____

_____

_____

_____

_____

_____

_____

_____

_____

_____

_____

_____

_____

_____

*"Love starts with me. I have to teach people how to love me
and hold them accountable because I'm worth it."*

ALICIA ADAMSON

_____

_____

_____

_____

_____

_____

_____

_____

_____

_____

_____

_____

_____

_____

_____

_____

_____

_____

_____

_____

_____

_____

"Stop lying about how you're really living — truth be told you are suffering in silence, dying inside, not wanting to reveal how you really feel about your life at this moment. You have permission to tell your truth and not look back again."

ALICIA ADAMSON

_____

_____

_____

_____

_____

_____

_____

_____

_____

_____

_____

_____

_____

_____

_____

_____

_____

_____

_____

_____

_____

_____

*"Fear is a real imaginary friend. It tries to convince you how real it is
and will try to cling to every new experience you want to do. I've learned to say,
"OK Fear, if you won't leave on your own, I'll just drag you along with me because
you're not going to stop me from going where I need to go.' "*

ALICIA ADAMSON

_____

_____

_____

_____

_____

_____

_____

_____

_____

_____

_____

_____

_____

_____

_____

_____

_____

_____

_____

_____

"Truth: You are equipped with everything you will ever need to face the successes and challenges in your life. If you just walk in who you are, you will win!"

ALICIA ADAMSON

_____

_____

_____

_____

_____

_____

_____

_____

_____

_____

_____

_____

_____

_____

_____

_____

_____

"Sometimes we have to love family members from afar.
If anyone interrupts our peace, they cannot stay."

ALICIA ADAMSON

_____

_____

_____

_____

_____

_____

_____

_____

_____

_____

_____

_____

_____

_____

_____

_____

_____

_____

_____

*"Every wound that has been healed, every tear that has been dried,
every need that has been met is all due to my personal relationship with God.
He has favored me and allowed me to have an abundant life.
My joy is because of Him only."*

ALICIA ADAMSON

WALKING IN YOUR TRUTH

"Life is intertwined, you cannot succeed in your professional life,
if you personally life is not solid and vice versa. I believe true authenticity comes
when there is a perfect intersection between your personal, spiritual and professional life.
That's the True you."

ALICIA ADAMSON

WALKING IN YOUR TRUTH

---

*"Truth is we all tell lies about who we are because we have been told we are
not good enough just the way we are. This world has no authority over you or your destiny.
You are free to authentically and unapologetically walk in your truth."*

ALICIA ADAMSON

_____

_____

_____

_____

_____

_____

_____

_____

_____

_____

_____

_____

_____

_____

_____

_____

_____

_____

_____

_____

_____

_____

"Sometimes you got to let the tears fall. They fall because you are grateful for the grace and mercy in your life. They fall to remind of you of just how far you have journeyed. They remind you that everything is going to be OK and that you are more than a conqueror, you are a survivor!"

ALICIA ADAMSON

Forgiveness = Freedom

ALICIA ADAMSON

_____

_____

_____

_____

_____

_____

_____

_____

_____

_____

_____

_____

_____

_____

_____

_____

_____

_____

_____

_____

_____

_____

_____

"The Truth Journey is lonely, you are unpacking along the way,
shedding off people and experiences that are not allowed on your destiny trip!
Stop trying to drag them along. This is your unique journey alone."

ALICIA ADAMSON

_____

_____

_____

_____

_____

_____

_____

_____

_____

_____

_____

_____

_____

_____

_____

_____

_____

_____

_____

_____

_____

*"Love starts with me. I have to teach people how to love me
and hold them accountable because I'm worth it."*

ALICIA ADAMSON

WALKING IN YOUR TRUTH

_____

_____

_____

_____

_____

_____

_____

_____

_____

_____

_____

_____

_____

_____

_____

_____

_____

_____

_____

_____

_____

_____

_____

_____

_____

*"Love starts with me. I have to teach people how to love me
and hold them accountable because I'm worth it."*

ALICIA ADAMSON

_____

_____

_____

_____

_____

_____

_____

_____

_____

_____

_____

_____

_____

_____

_____

_____

_____

_____

_____

_____

_____

_____

_____

"Stop lying about how you're really living — truth be told you are suffering in silence, dying inside, not wanting to reveal how you really feel about your life at this moment. You have permission to tell your truth and not look back again."

ALICIA ADAMSON

---

*"Fear is a real imaginary friend. It tries to convince you how real it is
and will try to cling to every new experience you want to do. I've learned to say,
"OK Fear, if you won't leave on your own, I'll just drag you along with me because
you're not going to stop me from going where I need to go.' "*

ALICIA ADAMSON

_____

_____

_____

_____

_____

_____

_____

_____

_____

_____

_____

_____

_____

_____

_____

_____

_____

_____

_____

_____

_____

_____

_____

"Truth: You are equipped with everything you will ever need to face the successes and challenges in your life. If you just walk in who you are, you will win!"

ALICIA ADAMSON

_____

_____

_____

_____

_____

_____

_____

_____

_____

_____

_____

_____

_____

_____

_____

_____

_____

_____

_____

_____

_____

_____

_____

"Sometimes we have to love family members from afar.
If anyone interrupts our peace, they cannot stay."

_____

_____

_____

_____

_____

_____

_____

_____

_____

_____

_____

_____

_____

_____

_____

_____

_____

_____

_____

_____

_____

_____

"Every wound that has been healed, every tear that has been dried,
every need that has been met is all due to my personal relationship with God.
He has favored me and allowed me to have an abundant life.
My joy is because of Him only."

ALICIA ADAMSON

WALKING IN YOUR TRUTH

_____

_____

_____

_____

_____

_____

_____

_____

_____

_____

_____

_____

_____

_____

_____

_____

_____

_____

_____

_____

_____

"Life is intertwined, you cannot succeed in your professional life,
if you personally life is not solid and vice versa. I believe true authenticity comes
when there is a perfect intersection between your personal, spiritual and professional life.
That's the True you."

ALICIA ADAMSON

WALKING IN YOUR TRUTH

_____

_____

_____

_____

_____

_____

_____

_____

_____

_____

_____

_____

_____

_____

_____

_____

_____

_____

_____

_____

_____

_____

*"Truth is we all tell lies about who we are because we have been told we are
not good enough just the way we are. This world has no authority over you or your destiny.
You are free to authentically and unapologetically walk in your truth."*

_____

_____

_____

_____

_____

_____

_____

_____

_____

_____

_____

_____

_____

_____

_____

_____

_____

_____

_____

_____

_____

_____

_____

_____

*"Sometimes you got to let the tears fall. They fall because you are grateful for
the grace and mercy in your life. They fall to remind of you of just how far you have journeyed.
They remind you that everything is going to be OK and that you are
more than a conqueror, you are a survivor!"*

ALICIA ADAMSON

Forgiveness = Freedom

ALICIA ADAMSON

_____

_____

_____

_____

_____

_____

_____

_____

_____

_____

_____

_____

_____

_____

_____

_____

_____

_____

_____

_____

_____

_____

_____

_____

*"The Truth Journey is lonely, you are unpacking along the way,
shedding off people and experiences that are not allowed on your destiny trip!
Stop trying to drag them along. This is your unique journey alone."*

ALICIA ADAMSON

_____

_____

_____

_____

_____

_____

_____

_____

_____

_____

_____

_____

_____

_____

_____

_____

_____

_____

_____

_____

_____

_____

_____

*"Love starts with me. I have to teach people how to love me
and hold them accountable because I'm worth it."*

ALICIA ADAMSON

_____

_____

_____

_____

_____

_____

_____

_____

_____

_____

_____

_____

_____

_____

_____

_____

_____

_____

_____

_____

_____

_____

_____

_____

*"Love starts with me. I have to teach people how to love me
and hold them accountable because I'm worth it."*

ALICIA ADAMSON

WALKING IN YOUR TRUTH

_____

_____

_____

_____

_____

_____

_____

_____

_____

_____

_____

_____

_____

_____

_____

_____

_____

_____

_____

_____

_____

_____

"Stop lying about how you're really living — truth be told you are suffering in silence, dying inside, not wanting to reveal how you really feel about your life at this moment. You have permission to tell your truth and not look back again."

ALICIA ADAMSON

_____

_____

_____

_____

_____

_____

_____

_____

_____

_____

_____

_____

_____

_____

_____

_____

_____

_____

_____

_____

_____

_____

_____

_____

*"Fear is a real imaginary friend. It tries to convince you how real it is
and will try to cling to every new experience you want to do. I've learned to say,
"OK Fear, if you won't leave on your own, I'll just drag you along with me because
you're not going to stop me from going where I need to go.' "*

ALICIA ADAMSON

_____
_____
_____
_____
_____
_____
_____
_____
_____
_____
_____
_____
_____
_____
_____
_____
_____
_____
_____

"Truth: You are equipped with everything you will ever need to face the successes and challenges in your life. If you just walk in who you are, you will win!"

ALICIA ADAMSON

_____

_____

_____

_____

_____

_____

_____

_____

_____

_____

_____

_____

_____

_____

_____

_____

_____

_____

_____

_____

_____

_____

_____

"Sometimes we have to love family members from afar.
If anyone interrupts our peace, they cannot stay."

ALICIA ADAMSON

_____

_____

_____

_____

_____

_____

_____

_____

_____

_____

_____

_____

_____

_____

_____

_____

_____

_____

_____

_____

_____

*"Every wound that has been healed, every tear that has been dried,
every need that has been met is all due to my personal relationship with God.
He has favored me and allowed me to have an abundant life.
My joy is because of Him only."*

ALICIA ADAMSON

WALKING IN YOUR TRUTH

"Life is intertwined, you cannot succeed in your professional life,
if you personally life is not solid and vice versa. I believe true authenticity comes
when there is a perfect intersection between your personal, spiritual and professional life.
That's the True you."

ALICIA ADAMSON

WALKING IN YOUR TRUTH

_____

_____

_____

_____

_____

_____

_____

_____

_____

_____

_____

_____

_____

_____

_____

_____

_____

_____

_____

_____

_____

_____

_____

_____

*"Truth is we all tell lies about who we are because we have been told we are
not good enough just the way we are. This world has no authority over you or your destiny.
You are free to authentically and unapologetically walk in your truth."*

_____

_____

_____

_____

_____

_____

_____

_____

_____

_____

_____

_____

_____

_____

_____

_____

_____

_____

_____

_____

_____

_____

*"Sometimes you got to let the tears fall. They fall because you are grateful for
the grace and mercy in your life. They fall to remind of you of just how far you have journeyed.
They remind you that everything is going to be OK and that you are
more than a conqueror, you are a survivor!"*

ALICIA ADAMSON

WALKING IN YOUR TRUTH

Forgiveness = Freedom

_____

_____

_____

_____

_____

_____

_____

_____

_____

_____

_____

_____

_____

_____

_____

_____

_____

_____

_____

_____

*"The Truth Journey is lonely, you are unpacking along the way,
shedding off people and experiences that are not allowed on your destiny trip!
Stop trying to drag them along. This is your unique journey alone."*

ALICIA ADAMSON

_____

_____

_____

_____

_____

_____

_____

_____

_____

_____

_____

_____

_____

_____

_____

_____

_____

_____

_____

_____

_____

_____

"Love starts with me. I have to teach people how to love me
and hold them accountable because I'm worth it."

_____

_____

_____

_____

_____

_____

_____

_____

_____

_____

_____

_____

_____

_____

_____

_____

_____

_____

_____

_____

_____

_____

_____

*"Love starts with me. I have to teach people how to love me
and hold them accountable because I'm worth it."*

ALICIA ADAMSON

WALKING IN YOUR TRUTH

_____

_____

_____

_____

_____

_____

_____

_____

_____

_____

_____

_____

_____

_____

_____

_____

_____

_____

_____

_____

_____

_____

_____

_____

_____

"Stop lying about how you're really living — truth be told you are suffering in silence, dying inside, not wanting to reveal how you really feel about your life at this moment. You have permission to tell your truth and not look back again."

---

*"Fear is a real imaginary friend. It tries to convince you how real it is
and will try to cling to every new experience you want to do. I've learned to say,
"OK Fear, if you won't leave on your own, I'll just drag you along with me because
you're not going to stop me from going where I need to go.""*

ALICIA ADAMSON

_____

_____

_____

_____

_____

_____

_____

_____

_____

_____

_____

_____

_____

_____

_____

_____

_____

_____

_____

_____

_____

_____

_____

_____

_____

"Truth: You are equipped with everything you will ever need to face the successes and challenges in your life. If you just walk in who you are, you will win!"

ALICIA ADAMSON

WALKING IN YOUR TRUTH

_____

_____

_____

_____

_____

_____

_____

_____

_____

_____

_____

_____

_____

_____

_____

_____

_____

_____

_____

_____

_____

"Sometimes we have to love family members from afar.
If anyone interrupts our peace, they cannot stay."

ALICIA ADAMSON

_____

_____

_____

_____

_____

_____

_____

_____

_____

_____

_____

_____

_____

_____

_____

_____

_____

_____

_____

*"Every wound that has been healed, every tear that has been dried,
every need that has been met is all due to my personal relationship with God.
He has favored me and allowed me to have an abundant life.
My joy is because of Him only."*

WALKING IN YOUR TRUTH

_____

_____

_____

_____

_____

_____

_____

_____

_____

_____

_____

_____

_____

_____

_____

_____

_____

_____

_____

_____

_____

_____

_____

*"Life is intertwined, you cannot succeed in your professional life,
if you personally life is not solid and vice versa. I believe true authenticity comes
when there is a perfect intersection between your personal, spiritual and professional life.
That's the True you."*

ALICIA ADAMSON

WALKING IN YOUR TRUTH

_____

_____

_____

_____

_____

_____

_____

_____

_____

_____

_____

_____

_____

_____

_____

_____

_____

_____

_____

_____

_____

_____

*"Truth is we all tell lies about who we are because we have been told we are
not good enough just the way we are. This world has no authority over you or your destiny.
You are free to authentically and unapologetically walk in your truth."*

ALICIA ADAMSON

WALKING IN YOUR TRUTH

_____

_____

_____

_____

_____

_____

_____

_____

_____

_____

_____

_____

_____

_____

_____

_____

_____

_____

_____

_____

_____

_____

"Sometimes you got to let the tears fall. They fall because you are grateful for the grace and mercy in your life. They fall to remind of you of just how far you have journeyed. They remind you that everything is going to be OK and that you are more than a conqueror, you are a survivor!"

ALICIA ADAMSON

_____
_____
_____
_____
_____
_____
_____
_____
_____
_____
_____
_____
_____
_____
_____
_____
_____
_____
_____
_____
_____
_____
_____
_____

Forgiveness = Freedom

_____

_____

_____

_____

_____

_____

_____

_____

_____

_____

_____

_____

_____

_____

_____

_____

_____

_____

_____

_____

_____

_____

_____

_____

"The Truth Journey is lonely, you are unpacking along the way,
shedding off people and experiences that are not allowed on your destiny trip!
Stop trying to drag them along. This is your unique journey alone."

Acknowledgments

Thanks be to God for creating me and using me for His glory and divine purpose! I'm grateful that you saved a wretch like me and that your grace and mercy are daily gifts not because of who I am but because of who you! I am honored and humbled to use my gifts to serve your people.

Thank you to my mother for being a pillar of strength and sacrificing your dreams just so your children could achieve theirs — they don't make them like you anymore. Ma, you made me who I am today. Thank you to my late Grandmother for always believing in her "glamour girl." You let me dream big. To my dad, you loved me when you didn't have to and gave me a glimpse of what a father and daughter relationship should be like and for that I thank you. To my husband, thank you for loving the real me and accepting everything that I am and not! Your strength and commitment to our marriage and our family breathes life into me and I'm a better person because of your love and friendship. To my sons — you both are the greatest gifts and challenge of my lifetime. Being your mom stretches me every day, sometimes I don't get it right but I will die trying to love you unconditionally and creating a world that you can thrive in. Thank you to my sisters Ledona and Cheyenne and my niece Charis for always challenging my ideals and my expressions of my truth!

Everyone needs special people who journey through life with you —
Thank you to my sister friends Wachmide, Nachelle, India, RaShonda, Ronisha, Shannon and Sharon —for always believing in me and supporting my evolution with good laughs along the way! Many thanks to my mentor and friend, Jaye, for teaching me to walk in my truth and growing with me since 19. To my wonderful editor and friend, Kimberly, thank you for helping to make this possible. Special thanks to Pastor Dickerson and Lady Dickerson at my church, Greater Love Tabernacle, for raising me to be a Bible believing, spirit-filled woman of God who is empowered to use her gifts in and outside of the church! And, to The National Black Women's Society (NBWS), thank you for continually supporting me and being a platform for strengthening the spirit of leadership in women.

To all of the women and men I've met over the years that I've shared long and short conversations with, short and long term relationships, you have made an impact. For all the open doors, speaking invitations, special opportunities and blessings I've had thus far, I'm grateful. I'm equally grateful for the hard lessons, broken promises, failed friendships, failures and disappointments- they have helped me grow in ways only experience could teach! *And we know that all things work together for good to those who love God, to those who are the called according to His purpose.* — Romans 8:28

I'm thankful for it all! I look forward to this next phase of higher heights and deeper depths. Thank you for letting me share my first published work with you.

From My Heart,

About the Author

For over a decade, Alicia has inspired hundreds of young women and men from all walks of life while serving as a guest speaker at conferences, local schools and universities, nonprofit organizations and churches and as founder emeritus of the National Black Women's Society, Inc. She has a true heart for women and young people and is committed to creating platforms for them to be inspired and empowered to live in truth. A Boston native, she has received local awards, honors and accolades for her leadership and contributions to Greater Boston through her alma mater, local media publications and the nonprofit sector. Alicia is currently pursuing her Masters in Divinity. This is her first literary work. She resides in Boston with her loving husband and two sons.

For more information, please visit aliciaadamson.org and follow Alicia on social media to keep the conversation going.

🅕 Alicia Adamson Author

🅣 @aliciacanady

#WALKINGINYOURTRUTH
ALICIAADAMSON.ORG

Are you hosting a conference, retreat, event, book club and would like to invite Alicia to speak and teach on Walking In Your Truth? Please contact walkinginyourtruth@gmail.com.

Want to go deeper? Join a small cohort of women the first weekend of November each year for an amazing weekend dedication to you. The Process is a weekend retreat for women who are seeking to understand their journey. Created and facilitated by Alicia, you don't want to miss this opportunity to invest in you.

Visit aliciaadamson.org for more information on how to register!